A Little B Cookbook

Rosamund Lambert

ILLUSTRATED BY SUE BENNETT-WILLIAMS

First published in 1990 by
The Appletree Press Ltd, 7 James Street
South, Belfast BT2 8DL. Text
© Rosamund Lambert, 1990. Illustrations © Sue
Bennett-Williams, 1990. Printed in the E.C. All
rights reserved. No part of this publication may
be reproduced or transmitted in any form
or by any means, electronic or mechanical,
photocopying, recording or any information
and retrieval system, without permission in
writing from the publisher.

British Library Cataloguing in Publication Data
Lambert, Rosamund
A little Bahamian cookbook.
1, Food, West Indian dishes – Recipes
I. Title
641.59729

ISBN 0-86281-234-8

9 8 7 6 5 4 3 2

Introduction

The cookery of the Bahamas has been influenced by many cultures – elements of the American south, the Caribbean, Britain, Spain and Africa have altered the course of Bahamian cuisine throughout history. This little book presents some of the islands' most popular and traditional dishes. Tomato-based dishes, featuring local seafood and meat, and with seasonings such as thyme and spicy hot peppers, are frequent and popular main courses, whilst native fruits and locally produced rum feature in local desserts and cocktails. The section at the end of this book describes some of the more obscure indigenous fruits of the Bahamas, together with their seasons and cooking uses.

Preparations for all the dishes are relatively simple and should not prove too time-consuming. By following substitution recommendations, it should be possible to re-create a taste of the Bahamas wherever you are.

A note on measures
Imperial, metric and American measures have been used in this book. Use one set of measures only as they are not necessarily exact equivalents. The cup referred to is the standard American measure, and spoon measures are level, not heaped. All recipes will serve four to six people.

Boil Fish

This delicious fish soup is a traditional breakfast dish and is reputed to be particularly efficacious after a late night! Serve with fresh Johnny Cake and grits for full effect.

---

2 lb/900 g grouper (or firm-fleshed white fish, e.g. monkfish or cod)
2 medium onions, sliced
4 oz/125 g/½ cup salt pork, diced
6 potatoes, quartered
2 limes
2 oz/50 g/¼ cup butter
⅔ pt/300 ml/1½ cup water

Cut the grouper into serving pieces and season with salt and pepper (and hot pepper, if desired). Place all the ingredients in a deep saucepan and simmer for 15-20 minutes. Add more water and adjust the seasoning, if required. Allow to cook over a medium heat for a further 15 minutes, or until the potatoes are cooked through. The fish should still be firm.

Johnny Cake

The origins of this simple, sweet bread are hazy; some say that the name derives from 'journey cake', the term used by spongers (the crew of ships employed in collecting

sponges) who prepared it over a small burner during long sea voyages. Traditionally served with Boil Fish, Johnny Cake is delicious warm and lightly buttered.

1½ lb/650 g/ 6 cups plain flour	2 tbsp sugar
	1 tsp salt
4 oz/100 g/⅔ cup lard or other shortening	water

Rub the shortening into the flour, then stir in the sugar and salt. Add enough water to make a dough and knead for about 2 minutes, or until the dough is smooth and cohesive. Shape into a round and place in a greased baking pan. Bake at gas mark 4, 350°F, 180°C until golden brown.

Grits

Also served with Boil Fish, grits are bleached cornmeal and when cooked are similar to semolina or porridge. This dish originated in the Southern states of America.

1½ pts/900 ml/3 cups water	6 oz/175 g/¾ cups grits
	¼ tsp salt

Stir the grits into boiling water, reduce the heat and cook for 3-5 minutes. Remove from the heat, cover and let the mixture stand to thicken. Serve topped with a knob of butter.

Conch Fritters

Conch (pronounced 'conk') fritters can be served as a starter or, smaller and on cocktail sticks, as hors d'oeuvres. If you are unable to obtain conch, canned tuna fish makes an excellent alternative.

---

4 fresh conchs, finely minced
1 large onion, finely chopped
1 green pepper, finely chopped
1 tbsp lime juice mixed in with hot pepper
1 tsp tomato ketchup (for colour)
1 large egg, beaten
1 tsp baking powder
1 tbsp flour
salt and pepper
hot pepper sauce

Mix all the ingredients together to form a sticky paste and adjust the seasonings to taste. Heat oil in a deep fryer or saucepan and when the oil is just smoking carefully drop in tablespoons of the mixture. Cook them until golden brown. Conch fritters can be prepared in advance and reheated before serving.

Prepare a cocktail sauce (blend 2 tbsp tomato ketchup, 1 tbsp mayonnaise, a squeeze of lemon or lime juice, salt and pepper and hot sauce to taste or 1 tsp horseradish sauce) and serve with the fritters.

Conch Chowder

Serve conch chowder in bowls or mugs and offer a dash of pepper sherry, which adds a zip to this already flavourful dish. You can substitute shrimp, if conch is not available.

---

2 oz/50 g/¼ cup salt pork or bacon, diced
6 conchs
2 onions, finely chopped
2 green peppers, diced
2 sticks of celery, finely sliced
3 potatoes, diced
2 oz/50 g/¼ cup tomato paste
5 medium-sized ripe tomatoes or 1 can peeled tomatoes

Beat the conchs until tender and then dice finely. Fry the salt pork until golden brown. Remove or leave, as desired, adding onions, peppers and celery to the pan. Cook until the liquid has almost all evaporated and pour in tomato paste and tomatoes. Add the diced conch. Bring to the boil and season to taste. Add sufficient water to cover and allow to simmer for 25 minutes, adjusting the water level if it becomes too dry.

Pepper Sherry Steep 6 whole hot peppers (or more, to taste) in a bottle of good-quality sherry for at least a month.

Pea Soup and Dough

Sometimes known as pea soup and dumpling, this thick and fragrant soup makes a hearty meal. If you cannot obtain salt beef, use stewing beef and cook for a little longer initially, until it is tender.

Soup

1 lb/450 g salt beef	2 celery stalks, diced
8 oz/225 g/2 cups pigeon peas	1 can peeled tomatoes
8 oz/225 g/1 cup salt pork, diced	4 tbsp tomato paste
2 onions, diced	thyme
1 sweet pepper, diced	salt and pepper
	hot pepper (optional)

Dough

4 oz/100 g/1 cup flour   ½ tsp salt   water

Cover the salt beef with water and boil for 15 minutes. Discard the water. Boil the pigeon peas in about 1 pt/500 ml/4 cups water until they are tender. In a frying pan, fry the salt pork and after a couple of minutes, add the onion, celery, sweet pepper and tomato paste. Simmer the mixture until it is pulpy and season to taste. Reheat the vegetable mixture with the peas, water and beef in a large saucepan. To make the dumplings, sift together the flour and salt and add enough water to make a stiff dough. Knead the dough briefly, roll it out and cut it into 1-inch squares. Add the squares to the soup one by one, to prevent sticking, and cook them for 15-30 minutes.

Smudder Grouper

The word 'smudder' is a derivation of 'smothered'. The quick cooking time retains the full flavour of the fish.

---

*2 medium-sized grouper fillets (or
other firm-fleshed white fish)
1 onion
1 green pepper
1 x 8 oz/250 g can tomatoes or
4 ripe tomatoes, skinned
thyme
salt and pepper
juice of half a lime*

Season the fish with salt, pepper and hot pepper (if desired) and sprinkle with lime juice. Place the fish in a baking dish and top with onion and pepper rings, crushed tomatoes and several sprigs of thyme. Bake for 20 minutes or until cooked through.

Steamed Pork Chops

This dish is best prepared using thin-cut loin pork chops.
It makes a simple and delicious family meal.

---

8 pork chops
2 medium onions, sliced
2 green peppers, sliced
1 clove garlic, crushed
2 x 8 oz/250 g cans tomatoes
3 tbsp tomato paste
thyme
salt and pepper
a few drops hot pepper sauce or
1 bird pepper, finely minced (optional)

Season the chops with flour and salt and pepper and
brown them in a little oil. When browned, remove them
from the pan with a slotted spoon. Fry the onions, garlic
and green peppers slowly until soft and return the chops
to the pan, adding the tomatoes, tomato paste and
thyme. Allow to boil for a couple of minutes. Season to
taste, lower the heat and simmer until the meat is tender,
about 45 minutes, adding more liquid if required.

Minced Crawfish

The warm Bahamian waters produce the Florida spiny lobster, known locally as crawfish. Most of the meat is found in the tail section. The shell can be used as a decorative individual serving dish. Any type of lobster can be used if crawfish is unavailable.

---

4 medium-sized crawfish tails
I large onion, diced
I clove garlic, crushed
4 tomatoes, diced or
I x 8 oz/250 g can tomatoes
2 tbsp tomato paste
thyme
hot pepper sauce (to taste)
salt and pepper

Place the crawfish tails in boiling water and cook until the meat is firm. Remove the crawfish from the pan, gently prise the meat from the shell and shred it with a fork. In a frying pan, fry the diced onions and garlic and add tomatoes, thyme and seasoning. When the mixture is simmering, add the shredded crawfish. Reduce the heat and cook gently until almost all the liquid has evaporated. Heap the meat into the shells and serve with Peas 'n Rice.

Bahama Fried Chicken

This is a popular dish throughout the islands. For a more healthy, but equally delicious result, you can bake the chicken instead of frying it.

---

1 chicken, jointed
2 eggs
2 tbsp evaporated milk
flour
bread or cracker crumbs
salt and pepper
hot pepper

Wash and dry the chicken pieces, carefully removing any excess fat. Season with salt, pepper and hot pepper (if desired). Beat together the eggs and evaporated milk. Dip the chicken first in flour, then in the egg mixture and lastly in crumbs. Either deep-fry or bake the chicken joints until they are golden brown.

Chicken Souse

You will often find pig's feet or sheep's tongue instead of chicken in a souse! Serve with grits and Johnny Cake (see pages 4 and 7).

---

1 medium-sized chicken, jointed
2 medium onions, sliced
2 cloves garlic, crushed
5 potatoes, peeled and quartered
4 carrots, scraped and thickly sliced
4 tbsp lime juice
1 oz/25 g/2 tbsp butter
allspice
1 bird pepper or
2 tbsp hot pepper sauce
water

Skin the chicken portions, if desired, and place them with the onions, garlic, potatoes, carrots, lime juice and butter in a large saucepan, adding sufficient water to cover. Break up the bird pepper and add it to the pan together with allspice to taste (about 6 berries should be sufficient). Bring to the boil and simmer for about 1 hour, or until the chicken falls off the bone and the potatoes are cooked through.

Cracked Conch

The beautiful conch shell is often taken home by visitors as a souvenir. The meat from the conch provides a staple in the Bahamian diet, cooked or raw, and this dish is one of the favourite ways of cooking with conch. Unfortunately, there is no real substitute for conch in this dish except possibly squid.

---

4 conchs
lime juice
2 eggs
flour
cracker or bread crumbs
salt and pepper
hot pepper to taste

Pound the conchs until the tendons are broken down and they are flattened to double size. Marinate them, covered in lime juice and hot pepper, for 1 hour. Do not refrigerate as this toughens the conch. Coat the conch pieces first in flour, then beaten egg and lastly in crumbs. Heat oil in a deep fryer or saucepan and when it is smoking add the conch and cook until it is golden brown, taking care not to overcrowd the pan. Remove the conch and drain it on a paper towel.

Grouper Fingers

Any firm white fish can be used in this Caribbean rendition of simple fish fingers.

---

2 medium-sized grouper fillets, cut into strips
lime juice
2 eggs, beaten
flour
breadcrumbs
Fried Plantain
2 plantains
salt and pepper
oil

Marinate the fish in lime juice, for 1 hour, seasoned with hot pepper if desired. Dredge the fish in flour, then egg and lastly in crumbs. Refrigerate it for 10 minutes. Heat oil in a deep fryer or saucepan until it begins to smoke and cook the fish strips until they are golden brown. Garnish them with lemon or lime wedges and serve with fried plantain and coleslaw.

Fried Plantain Slice the plantains lengthwise then quarter the slices and season them with salt and pepper. Heat oil until it begins to smoke and deep-fry the plantain slices until they are golden brown.

Peas 'n Rice

Peas 'n Rice, in one form or another, can be found throughout the Caribbean. In the Bahamas, it is made with pigeon peas and is served alongside most entrées. If necessary, blackeye peas or even kidney beans can be used as a substitute for pigeon peas.

---

2 oz/50 g/¼ cup salt pork or bacon, diced
1 small onion, minced
1 green pepper, diced
1 stick celery, diced
1 x 8 oz/250 g can pigeon peas
4 tbsp tomato paste
1 cup rice
2 cups water
thyme

Fry the salt pork until it is crisp. Add the onion, green pepper and celery and cook until the mixture is pulpy. Add tomato paste and cook until most of the liquid in the pan has evaporated. Add the drained pigeon peas, thyme, salt and pepper and cook for a further 2 minutes. Pour in the rice and add water to cover. Cover the pot tightly and allow the mixture to simmer until all the liquid has evaporated.

Macaroni

Bahamian macaroni is cooked into solid cake form and cut into squares. It complements most entrées.

---

8 oz/225 g/2 cups macaroni
1 onion, diced
1 green pepper, diced
4 oz/100 g/1 cup grated strong Cheddar cheese
2 eggs, beaten
1 can evaporated milk
hot pepper
pinch of sugar
paprika

Boil the macaroni until tender, and soften the onion and green pepper in water. Drain them and place with the macaroni in a baking tray. Mix in the cheese, egg and evaporated milk. Season to taste, adding a pinch of sugar for extra flavour. Sprinkle the top with a little extra cheese and paprika and bake at gas mark 4, 350°F, 180°C for 20 minutes or until the mixture has set firm.

Coleslaw

Although only Bahamian by adoption, coleslaw is an enduring local favourite, served alongside most entrées. Spice it up with peppers, to taste.

---

1 head cabbage, shredded
2 lb/900 g/4 cups carrots, shredded
2 large onions, finely diced
¼ pt/150 ml/½ cup mayonnaise
2 tsp lemon or lime juice
2 tsp sugar
salt and pepper
hot pepper

Mix all the ingredients together and season to taste. Refrigerate the mixture for 1 hour before serving.

Coconut Cream Pie

Coconuts grow in abundance in the islands and are used both in desserts and cocktails.

Pastry

8 oz/250 g/2 cups flour	2 tbsp butter
4 oz/125 g/½ cup shortening	pinch of salt
	iced water

Filling

8 oz/250 g/2 cups grated fresh coconut	6 oz/175 g/¾ cup sugar
¾ pt/500 ml/2 cups evaporated milk	3 tbsp cornstarch (cornflour)
⅓ pt/250 ml/1 cup water	4 eggs, separated
	1 tsp vanilla essence

Meringue Topping

4 egg whites reserved from filling

6 tbsp sugar

4 oz/125 g/½ cup coconut, toasted

Sift together the flour and salt and cut in the butter and shortening until the mixture resembles fine breadcrumbs. Add sufficient water to form a cohesive dough and knead lightly until smooth. Chill the dough for 15 minutes in the refrigerator, then roll it out on a floured board to fit an 8- or 9-inch pie dish. Bake blind at gas mark 4, 350°F, 180°C until golden brown. Place the evaporated milk and half of the water in the top section of a double boiler. In a separate bowl, mix the remaining water, egg yolks, cornstarch, vanilla and sugar. Slowly add this mixture to the milk and water and cook over a medium heat, stirring constantly, until it has slightly thickened. Blend in the coconut well. When the mixture has thickened, pour it carefully into the prepared pie crust. Beat the egg whites with the salt until they are stiff and add sugar one tablespoon at a time, beating thoroughly between additions. Continue beating until the meringue forms stiff peaks. Gently pour the meringue over the pie and sprinkle with toasted coconut. Bake at gas mark 4, 350°F, 180°C, until meringue is lightly browned.

Bahama Bananas Flambé

Three essentially Caribbean ingredients – bananas, dark rum and brown sugar – are combined in this easy dessert.

4 bananas, just ripe	2 oz/50 g/¼ cup breadcrumbs
juice of 3 oranges	
8 fl oz/250 ml/1 cup rum	2 oz/50 g/¼ cup butter
2 tbsp brown sugar	flaked almonds (optional)

Slice the bananas lengthwise and place them in an ovenproof dish. Cover them with the orange juice, half the rum and the sugar. Sprinkle the breadcrumbs evenly over the bananas, dot with butter and cover the dish with a lid or foil. Bake at gas mark 4, 350°F, 180°C, for about ½ hour. When the bananas are ready, sprinkle almonds on top and heat the remaining rum in a small pan. At the

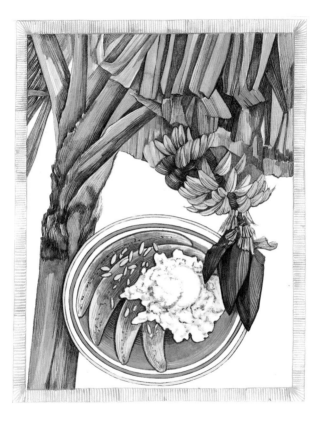

table pour the rum over the bananas and carefully flamber. Serve with whipped cream or ice cream.

Guava Duff

Duffs can be made using mango, pineapple, or even coconut and raisins. Hard Sauce is an essential accompaniment.

---

12 medium-sized guavas (about 1 lb/450 g)	6 oz/175 g/¾ cup shortening
1 tsp ground cinnamon	3 tsp baking powder
1 tsp ground allspice	1 tsp salt
2 tbsp sugar	¼ pt/150 ml/½ cup milk
1 lb/450 g/4 cups flour	1 egg, beaten
Hard Sauce	
6 oz/150 g/¾ cup sugar	2 eggs
8 oz/225 g/1 cup butter	brandy or rum to taste

Wash, peel and halve the guavas. Remove the seeds and strain them through a sieve. Set the juice aside. Cook the diced fruit gently with the spices and sugar until soft. Sift together the flour, baking powder and salt and cut in the shortening until the mixture resembles breadcrumbs. Add milk and egg and mix to a soft dough. Next, either add the fruit to the dough and knead the mixture until it is smooth or, alternatively, knead the dough, roll it out into a large rectangle and spread the fruit on top. In either case, roll up the dough from the short end and wrap it in cloth or foil. Cook in a double boiler for at least 1 hour.

Hard Sauce Cream the butter and sugar. Add the eggs one by one and beat vigorously until blended. Beat in brandy or rum until the sauce is smooth. Chill.

Rum Cake

Rum is made locally and transforms this simple cake into a special-occasion dessert, rich, dense and sinfully good.

1 lb/450 g/4 cups plain flour, sifted	½ pt/250 ml/1 cup milk
	5 tbsp dark rum
4 oz/125 g/½ cup butter	1 tsp vanilla essence
4 oz/125 g/½ cup sugar	2 oz/50 g/½ cup raisins
4 eggs	2 oz/50 g/½ cup
2 tsp baking powder	chopped nuts

Glaze

6 oz/175 g/¾ cup sugar	6 fl oz/150 ml/½ cup dark rum
3 fl oz/75 ml/¼ cup water	½ tsp vanilla
4 oz/125 g/½ cup butter	

Preheat the oven to gas mark 3, 325°F, 170°C. Grease and flour a tube or bundt pan and line the base with chopped nuts. Cream together the butter and sugar until fluffy, beating in the eggs one at a time. Mix in flour and milk alternately, ending with flour. Add rum, vanilla and raisins. Pour mixture carefully into the pan and bake for about 1 hour. Invert the cake on a rack and allow to cool. Return it to the pan before glazing.

Glaze Boil the water and sugar together for 3-5 minutes. Remove the pan from the heat and add the rum and vanilla. Pierce the cake with a skewer several times and dribble the glaze over the top and between the cake and the sides of the pan. Store cake in the pan.

Eleuthera Pineapple Tart

Pineapples grown on the beautiful island of Eleuthera in the central Bahamas are used in this popular treat.

---

1 lb/450 g/4 cups crushed pineapple
8 oz/225 g/1 cup sugar
8 oz/225 g/2 cups plain flour
6 oz/175 g/¾ cup butter or shortening, cubed
3 tbsp ice-cold water
pinch of salt

Simmer the pineapple and sugar together for 15-20 minutes, then leave the mixture to cool. Sift the flour and salt and cut in the butter until the mixture resembles breadcrumbs. Blend in two tablespoons of water and mix to a firm dough, adding more water if necessary. Knead the dough lightly for a few minutes, until it is smooth and firm. Chill it in the refrigerator for 10 minutes and then roll it out evenly to fit a 9-inch baking pan, reserving some pastry for the top. Pour in the filling. Cut strips of pastry and make a lattice top. Bake the tart at gas mark 4, 350°F, 180°C, for 1 hour or until the pastry is golden brown.

Coconut Tart Simmer 2 cups of grated coconut, 1 cup of sugar, nutmeg and mace to taste, and 2 cups of water until the mixture is almost dry. Spread this filling over the pastry and bake as above.

Benny Cake

'Benny' is the local name for sesame seeds and this candy has a lovely nutty flavour, complemented by a hint of orange. You will often find this sweet treat at fairs and streetside vendors' stalls.

---

8 oz/225 g/½ cup benny seeds
8 oz/225 g/½ cup white sugar
8 oz/225 g/½ cup soft brown sugar
½ pt/125 ml/½ cup water
peel of one orange, finely chopped

Parch the benny seeds in a dry frying-pan over a medium heat, stirring constantly, until just golden. In a saucepan simmer the benny, sugars, orange peel and water until the mixture coats the back of a spoon and is golden brown. Drop tablespoonfuls of the mixture onto a greased and dampened baking tray and allow to set in a cool, dry place.

Guava Jelly

Guavas come into season in October to November. When making this jelly, best results are achieved by using just-ripe fruit and avoiding any which appear bruised. Try spreading guava jelly on Johnny Cake for a delicious breakfast or snack.

---

2 lb/900 g/4 cups ripe guavas, halved
sugar
lemon juice

Quarter the guavas and place them in a heavy-duty pan with enough water to cover them. Bring the liquid to the boil and simmer for half an hour. Strain the guavas through a jelly or muslin bag, discarding the fruit when all the juice is extracted. Take care not to squeeze the fruit too hard. If you do, the juice will take on a bitter flavour. Return the juice to the pan and bring to the boil with 4 oz/100 g/1 cup of sugar per cup of juice, stirring occasionally. Add 1 teaspoon of lemon juice per cup of juice and continue to cook the mixture over a medium heat until it becomes syrupy and coats the back of a spoon. Allow it to cool for 10 minutes and then pour it carefully into sterilised jars. Seal well.

Cocktails

Let us set the scene – a coral sunset on a balmy evening with the breeze rustling through the palm fronds, carrying the scent of the sea. Cocktails are served:

Banana Daiquiri Bursting with the rich flavour of bananas, this daiquiri is served thick and frosty. Daiquiris are made with other fruits too, such as strawberries, mangoes and limes.

Place in an electric blender 4 ripe, peeled bananas, I measure of light rum, I measure of banana liqueur, a ½ measure of sugar syrup, a squeeze of lime and fill up the blender with cracked ice. Blend. Adjust the flavourings to taste.

Goombay Smash Goombay was a form of Bahamian music, the forerunner of calypso, and was synonymous with happy times. This cocktail certainly fits the bill.

Place in a shaker I measure of dark rum, a ½ measure of coconut rum, a dash of sugar syrup and lemon juice and top this up with pineapple juice. Shake the mixture well and pour it into a glass of cracked ice.

Bahama Mama Nassau Royale is a locally produced liqueur tasting of vanilla.

Place in a shaker I measure of dark rum, a ½ measure of Nassau Royale, and a dash of lemon juice and fill the shaker up with a mix of orange, pineapple and lime juices (fruit punch). Shake the cocktail well and pour it into a glass of cracked ice. Top with a maraschino cherry.

Bahamian Coffee

Bahamian coffee is a delicious way to round off a good meal.

---

1 measure dark rum
¾ measure Nassau Royale liqueur
pot of hot, strong coffee
whipped cream

Dip the rim of several tall, stemmed glasses in rum and then in sugar to coat. Pour coffee, rum and liqueur into the glasses and top with whipped cream.

Sour sop

Sugar apple

Soursop

The soursop is closely related to the sugar apple. The fruit is quite large and quite irregular in shape. The exterior is dark green, which turns blackish when fully ripe, and covered in soft spines, where the carpels have not developed as in the sugar apple. The flesh is more strongly flavoured than that of the sugar apple and less sweet and there are many black seeds throughout. Sour sops are delicious in ice cream, daiquiris, jams and as flavouring for cakes.

Sugar Apple

Also known as sweetsop, the sugar apple is grown to a limited extent in the Caribbean and Southern states of America. The fruit resembles a pine cone in shape, with carpels which protrude and which are not completely fused. On the inside the pulp is creamy white, custard-like in consistency and very sweet. Each protuberance or segment contains a large black seed. Sugar apples are in season during the summer months. They are used in making ice creams.

Sapodilla

Known locally as 'dillies', sapodillas originated in central America, but grow very well in the warmth of the Bahamas. The tree is the source of chicle, which forms the basis for chewing gum. The brownish-looking fruit resembles kiwi fruit on the exterior and the flesh is reddish-brown and fragrantly sweet to the taste. There are up to 12 shiny black seeds in each fruit and the flesh, when fully ripe, can be used for compotes, ice cream or jam.

"Billy"

Sapodilla

Goat Peppers

Bird Peppers

Hot Peppers

Goat Pepper · Bird Pepper

Beware, the faint-hearted – both these peppers are miniature incendiary devices, to be handled with care! Both are available most of the year round and are used in many savoury dishes. The bird pepper, which ranges in colour from orange to bright red, has a little more juice than the goat pepper, which is pale orange, but they are equally fiery. Bahamians like spicy food and both peppers are used to season fish and meats, or are mashed in lime juice as a marinade or served in a sauce for dishes such as Cracked Conch or Grouper Fingers.

Breadfruit

The breadfruit tree is found throughout the tropics and the fruit, which is treated as a vegetable, is large and oblong with a knobbly green exterior. In the Bahamas, breadfruit are in season during the summer months. The flesh is fairly bland, similar to potatoes, and can be served sliced and fried gently in oil until soft, or boiled and then mashed with butter, to accompany any main dish, such as steamed pork chops or Smudder Grouper.

Breadfruit

Index